a harbour

Lorna Rice

BookLeaf
Publishing

India | USA | UK

Presentation by *BookLeaf Publishing*

Web: www.bookleafpub.com

E-mail: info@bookleafpub.com

ISBN: 9789357215480

First edition 2022

For Atlas, Fae, and Zephyr

For Nanny

an ode to overthinking

the clasping of fear is palpable
organs race with an attempt to medicate
and so I placate with the lure of promise;
A calming smoke for the nerves

but the ship has sailed long before the first
inhale;
fantastical fears with little foothold in reality
habitually overthinking on empty, a light on red
the time is wasted, but still I cannot think any
less

age

the rough wind tears through sails and bones
without distinction;
I shiver, a chill courses through sheets of flesh,
and I never wear layers enough.
A raging sea frantically pounds; hostile to a land
more ragged than I remember
and the seagulls mew at it, as if to provoke an
incensed assault –
with the sharpness of their cries filed within a
recollection somewhere,
and through the same eyes do I see - but older
than the eyes which have gone before

petrichor

3

Petrichor, sweet air
After rain and heat collide -
Breathe deep, little one

reverie

Dusk, and the slip into reverie
intoxicated by the sweetest dreams; a breeze of
lucidity - and I breathe you in the deepest -
the web of time folds into the warmest white –
you're but a sigh in my mind,
and I won't speak a word of it

the zephyr on a balmy day,
the windswept tidal wave washing season into
season,
a reverie, winter skies, and the little girl who
dreamed dreams of magic sweeping her away,
if you chose to be seen, I could not look
anywhere else

wayfarer

5

The one who walks
The one who walks so as not to wait
The one who waits so as not to jump
The one who jumps so as not to miss
The one who misses so as not to take
The one who takes so as not to lose

The one who wanders
The one who wanders so as not to wonder
The one who wonders so as not to feel the still
The one who walks and wanders in circles to
elude thinking at all,
too many feedback loops cutting in, cutting in

disembodied

6

I ache to not tear the skin away,
but perhaps something will feel better within
me,
I cling to regrets,
but do not feel any better for having them

I long to feel beautiful,
but beautiful I am not,
as you have reminded me so many times,
that I do not look like other girls

onism

Tales on screens and in dreams; my Pinterest is
somebody else's reality
longing for the lives of those who may wish for
mine,
to trade places but for a second, yet so impeded
by emotion too mighty to let up -
and when the four walls boxing in the soul begin
to feel too small,
if I fear I might suffocate here, I'll dip my toes
into a dream;
there's a favourite of a cabin, and a fire, by a
lake, which I like -
I do wonder if anyone else drowns themselves in
unnecessary complexities,
somewhat rotting in their own experience
we are who we are until the end

winter solstice

8

Crisp leaves, fire dancing -
Hold me tight, so very tight
On the longest night

half

If existential fragility absolves dishonesty -
will we happily fold into our intoxications and
our grief?
The skies and the trees ask so little of me -
yet the synchronicities do not let me sleep
and I do not remember asking for this

Sometimes I write letters,
demanding to know why every breath clings to
its belief system;
water my morals daily, uphold what is expected
of me
but still I am unsure of what this is, and too
afraid to ask

Who am I? And who are you?
Inclined to catastrophise wildly,
and why are you at the forefront so suddenly?
It's all an imagining, I think. I think?

It's frustrating, disintegrating into half of what
was
a half and not a whole,
while finding it richly satisfying and
intoxicating,

and some days the melancholy is so invasive I
cannot eat
did not ask for this, do not want it, I only asked
to be free

No one can turn my mind inside out like I can,
any distraction will do, so the mess in my chest
aches less
but the ache is a chasm, and the chasm is you
there is no reason, and I didn't ask for this

the Summer Buddy

Sonder, and the need to wander, meander,
under cornflower skies, with a pup through the
lanes
Ben Howard and the melancholia again,
'sage that she was burning' plays
the heat hits in that comforting way,
nostalgia and haze fizz and fight for their place
till we hit the fields, the sea is lit from the sun,
and here, the pup rolls in some mud, with a grin
we find our spot to sit – basking like snakes in
the heat
Ben lulls to a stop, I light up, and we watch the
birds

skin

Born into skin ill-fitting
lately have felt less than myself
dreams I have dreamed went their separate
ways,
is there something wrong with me?

Try to be a little quieter on the inside
the fight to present just right
don't know how to say hello when I'm anxious,
who do I have to be so weird?

Most myself when I feel free,
still brittle but with a warmth deeper down
societal ice is thin and unforgiving
keeping two steps behind for safety

king

The riddle wearing a pleasant expression;
but liar is not the face you are wearing
hide your hands, should they reveal something
snakes shed skin; one for each mood you are in,
I lose track of them
but nobody else sees

yearn

14

In the sitting in my house,
in the longing to be elsewhere
as if pulled, a want to be outside
it rains here, but I do not mind

I know of a bench to sit,
my preferred place to watch the sea
the clock chimes;
exhale into the following year

tiny

15

Tiny fingers and tiny toes, eyes shut tight
who will you be? I wonder
I know not how to keep another person alive,
in the temporary house, in the temporary life
but we sit tight, you and I,
warm blankets and nursing through long nights;
you have blue eyes, wide-eyed
and you take me in for a little bit, till the nap
calls

bloom

Sweet like the sweet pea
Adoring of the morning -
Bloom for a short time

autumn '16

17

Opium, speed and autumn leaves
Poets of the fall, little sleep, worse dreams
twenty-one into twenty-two, watching boats
until the dusk falls upon you,
the night-time walks to the quay, lights
twinkling

niceties, pleasantries, and I'm complimenting
your art
think this is where I discovered my
homesickness for Mars -
I definitely had a dream about it once
Go to work, then I wake up - another dance in
the dark

blood

Your years disappear
mine blinked to almost thirty, somewhere
you created the blank page, now teach it
something
your blood who you claim to love,
but you love the drink, too

To mourn the lost time you designed,
I had hoped for an easier life
we share blood, well aware of the passing of
time
please just have a conversation with me,
I long to know what we share

spectre

19

Quite disquieting it is, though I'll turn my head
till you fade
We do not speak in words; you prefer it that
way, as do I
The spectre on mute, but what could have been
had with you?
Sit in our distinct bubbles and exist like this, for
a time

www.ingramcontent.com/pod-product-compliance
Lightning Source LLC
Chambersburg PA
CBHW070740160726
48003CB00006BA/2564